AMERICAN JOURNEY

A Treasury of Rand McNally Road Atlas Covers
1924 - 2019

Published in U.S.A.
Printed in Canada

ISBN 10: 0-528-02035-8
ISBN 13: 978-0-528-02035-3

For licensing information and copyright permissions,
contact us at permissions@randmcnally.com
If you have a comment, suggestion, or even a compliment,
please visit us at randmcnally.com/contact or write to
Rand McNally Consumer Affairs
P.O. Box 7600
Chicago, Illinois 60680-9915

1 2 3 TC 20 19 18

Contents

While reading through this book, you may notice multiple *Road Atlas* covers for individual years. Rand McNally has a long tradition of publishing specialty atlases as well as customized covers, some of which are represented in this anthology.

THE JOURNEY BEGINS

When William Rand opened his commercial print shop at 148 West Lake Street in Chicago, he advertised "every description of printing, on the most advantageous terms." It was 1856. Two years later, Andrew McNally, recently arrived from Ireland, entered into Rand's shop, inquired about a job, and was hired on the spot for $9 a week.

When the two men met, they couldn't have imagined how their business would grow – from printing railroad tickets and timetables to publishing a full line of educational maps, geography textbooks, and globes (1880s); road maps and guides (early 1900s); and the best-selling *Road Atlas* (1924).

When the first *Road Atlas* debuted, particular attention was paid to the cover art. Each cover thereafter communicates not only the freedom that an atlas represents but the inspiration it provides in moving people to take to the roads in search of adventure.

THE
1920s

A new standard of living. A time of prosperity.
Modernity for the masses.

From art to music to moving pictures to automobiles, the 1920s roared
with excitement and adventure – fueled by a booming economy. Driving was
an affordable luxury, with a range of autos for every income.
Thanks to automobiles, there were new jobs in the oil fields, auto service
shops, roadside restaurants – and new opportunities for mapmakers.

During the initial years of the Rand McNally *Road Atlas*, the cover art
reflects the 1920s as a time of leisure and touring with a focus on
Model Ts and other early automobiles.

American realism was a popular art style of the time. *Road Atlas* covers
depicted aspirational scenes realistically drawn to showcase the
accessibility and possibility of adventure for everyone out on the road.

ROADSIDE ATTRACTION

In 1924, June McCarroll of
Indio, California persuaded the
California Highway Commission
to paint white center lines down
3,500 miles of highway to establish
lane widths and increase road safety.
Five years prior, McCarroll had
been run off the road by a truck
while driving her Model T.

1926

1927

1928

1929

THE
1930s

An economic downturn. Roads of opportunity.
The age of machinery.

American life went from boom to bust with the crash of the stock
market in 1929. Building more roads became part of the federal plan
for boosting the economy during the Great Depression. By 1939 there were
nearly 1.4 million miles of paved road in America – and plenty of new gas
stations, garages, motels, and restaurants to cater to drivers' needs.

The decade also was an age of machines, of automobile assembly lines, and
metalworking. The new roads facilitated a nationwide distribution of goods.

The graphic design style of the day is reflected in the *Road Atlas* covers.
Tempered colors, curved shapes, and bold lines defined the 1930s deco
with a sense of movement and scale that spoke to a better future and the
accessibility of modern machinery like the automobile.

ROADSIDE ATTRACTION

By 1930, 23 million cars were
on the road. In1935, only 39
of the 48 states required drivers to
have a license, although few
of those states required drivers
to take a test. New drivers often
turned to their auto dealers,
associations such as the YMCA,
and family and friends, for
driving lessons.

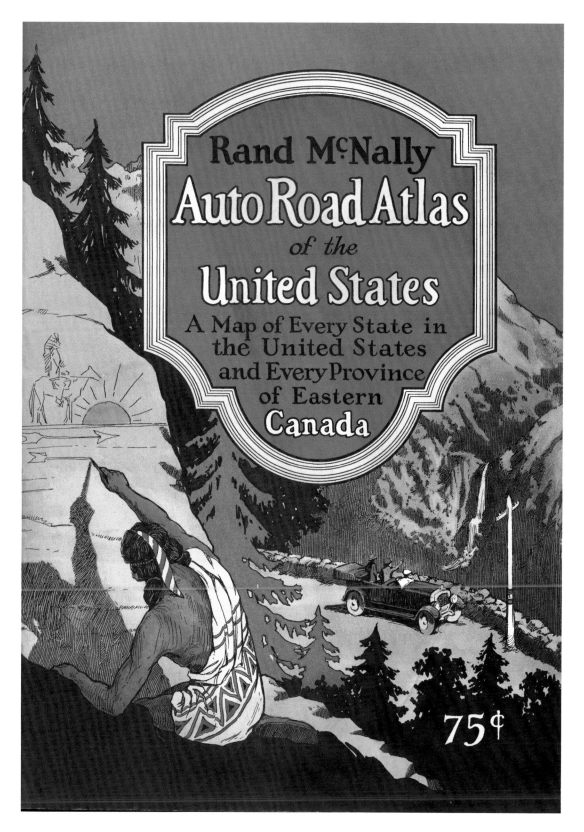

1931

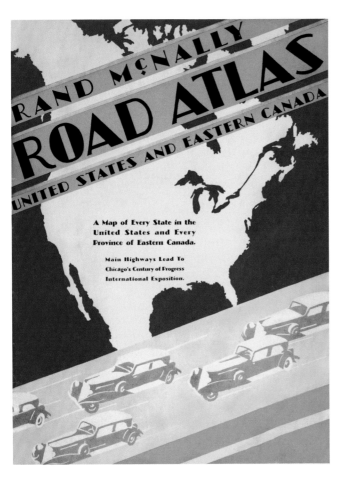

1932

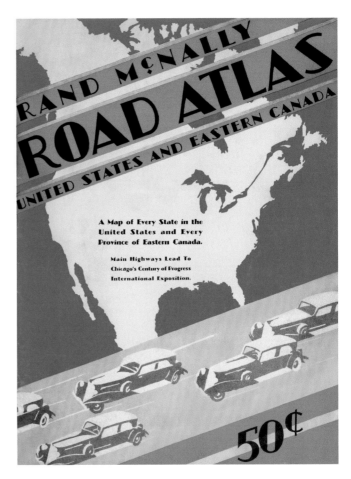

1933

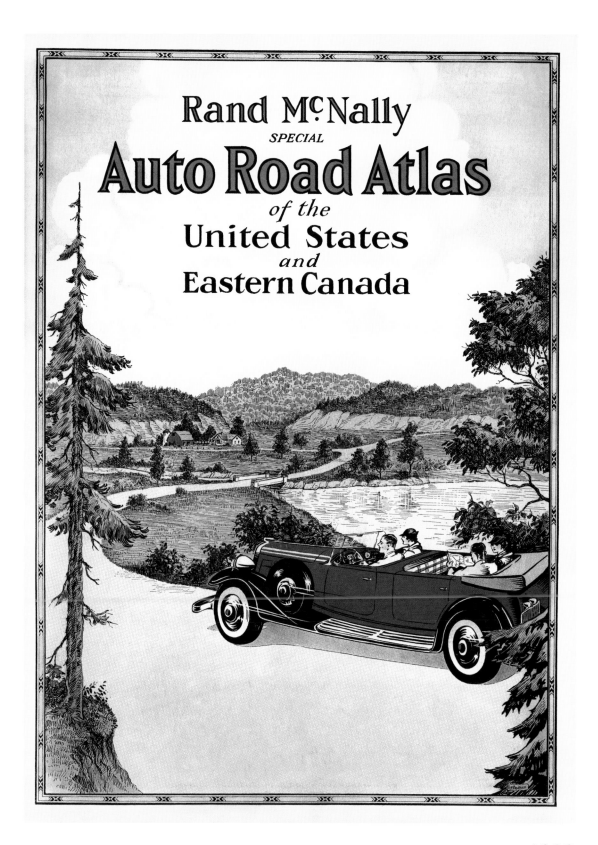

1933

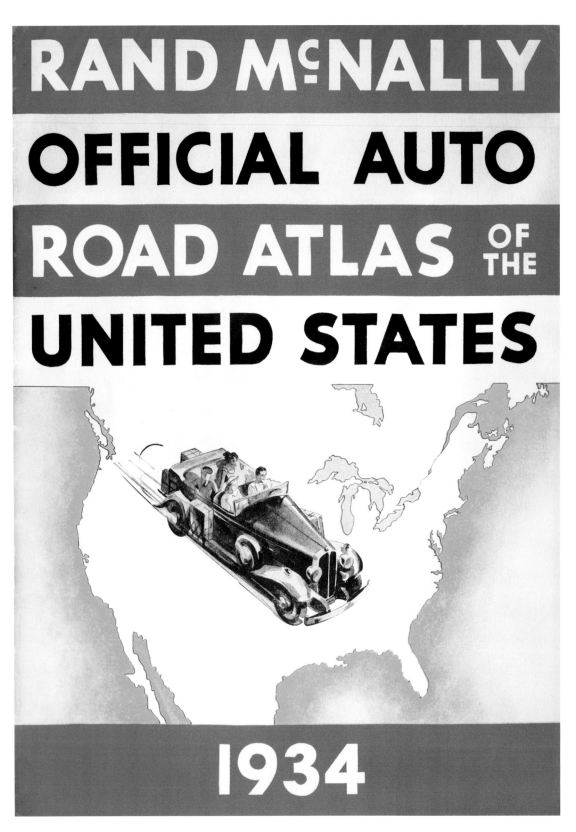

RAND McNALLY

OFFICIAL AUTO

ROAD ATLAS OF THE

UNITED STATES

1934

1934

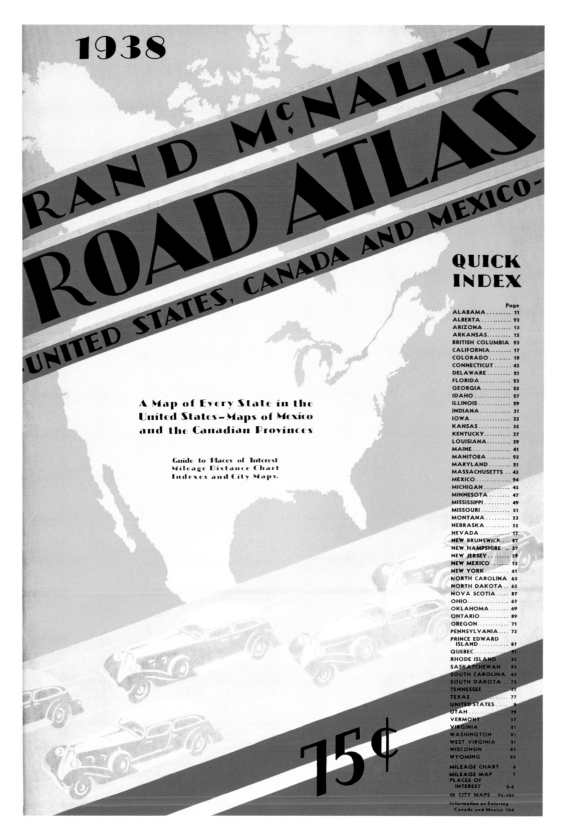

1938

RAND McNALLY
ROAD ATLAS
UNITED STATES, CANADA AND MEXICO-

A Map of Every State in the
United States — Maps of Mexico
and the Canadian Provinces

Guide to Places of Interest
Mileage Distance Chart
Indexes and City Maps.

QUICK INDEX

75¢

1938

THE
1940s

World War II. Travel halted. Recovery to prosperity.

The year 1940 began with the opening of the Pennsylvania Turnpike and flourishing prospects for modern highway design. However, within months of the attack on Pearl Harbor - December 7, 1941- road construction, automobile production, and map publishing all but stopped. During the war, gasoline was tightly rationed, causing families to cut driving in favor of public transportation.

Postwar, in the second half of the decade, the demand for new cars to accommodate business and leisure travel erupted. Purchasing and driving station wagons, sedans, and sports cars became a way to reflect recovery and project social standing.

Graphic design also felt the war's impact. Early 1940s *Road Atlas* covers continued deco designs, and then became more somber with the times. After 1945, however, designs were more optimistic and abstract, with rich but minimal color palettes that suggest sunnier times ahead.

ROADSIDE ATTRACTION

In 1946, after serving in World War II, the songwriter Bobby Troup traveled Route 66 from Pennsylvania to California. Inspired while driving, he penned the song "(Get Your Kicks on) Route 66," romanticizing many of the road's stops. Initially recorded by Nat King Cole, the song has been recorded by many artists, including the Rolling Stones.

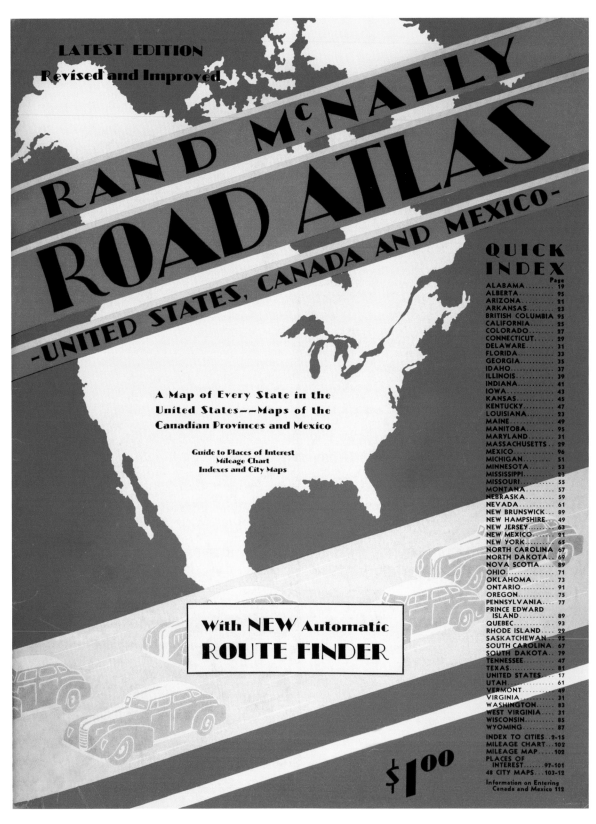

LATEST EDITION
Revised and Improved

RAND McNALLY
ROAD ATLAS
–UNITED STATES, CANADA AND MEXICO–

A Map of Every State in the
United States——Maps of the
Canadian Provinces and Mexico

Guide to Places of Interest
Mileage Chart
Indexes and City Maps

With **NEW** Automatic
ROUTE FINDER

$1.00

1942

RAND McNALLY
Special ROAD ATLAS

UNITED STATES · CANADA · MEXICO

1949

THE
1950s

Family cars. The 'burbs. The birth of the interstate.

After World War II, automobiles and new highways enabled the building of the modern American suburb – complete with drive-in restaurants. A prewar plan to connect America's cities via high-speed highways became a reality – changing lives, landscapes, and maps as families in station wagons took to the road.

The Federal-Aid Highway Act of 1956, enacted by President Eisenhower, provided the money and workforce to build a modern, 41,000-mile network of interstate highways.

The modern roads complemented the 1950s design styles of mid-century modern, international, and Bauhaus. From the cars people drove to the Rand McNally *Road Atlases* that guided them, design was clean with simple lines, limited colors, and artistic typefaces.

ROADSIDE ATTRACTION

Numbers of U.S. Interstate Highways indicate the direction the roads take. Odd-numbered routes run north-south, and even-numbered routes run east-west. The longest route is I-90, between Seattle and Boston, 3,020.54 miles. The shortest is I-97, between Annapolis and Baltimore, 17.62 miles. I-95 crosses sixteen states.

1950

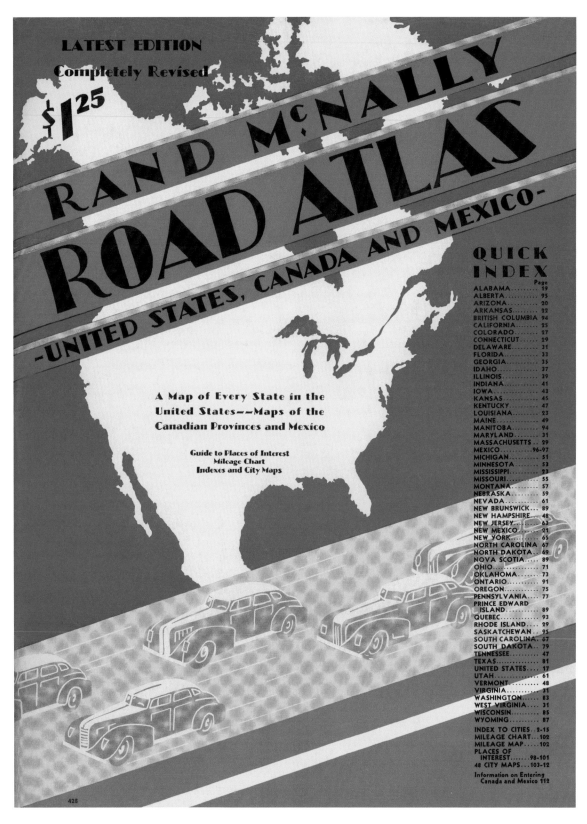

LATEST EDITION

Completely Revised

$1²⁵

RAND McNALLY ROAD ATLAS

-UNITED STATES, CANADA AND MEXICO-

A Map of Every State in the
United States~~Maps of the
Canadian Provinces and Mexico

Guide to Places of Interest
Mileage Chart
Indexes and City Maps

428

1950

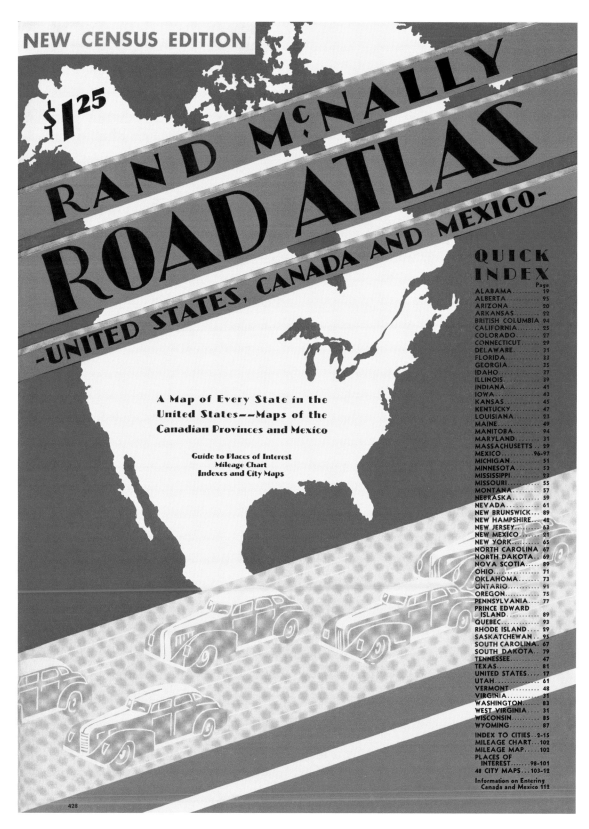

NEW CENSUS EDITION

$1²⁵

RAND McNALLY
ROAD ATLAS
-UNITED STATES, CANADA AND MEXICO-

A Map of Every State in the
United States~~Maps of the
Canadian Provinces and Mexico

Guide to Places of Interest
Mileage Chart
Indexes and City Maps

428

1951

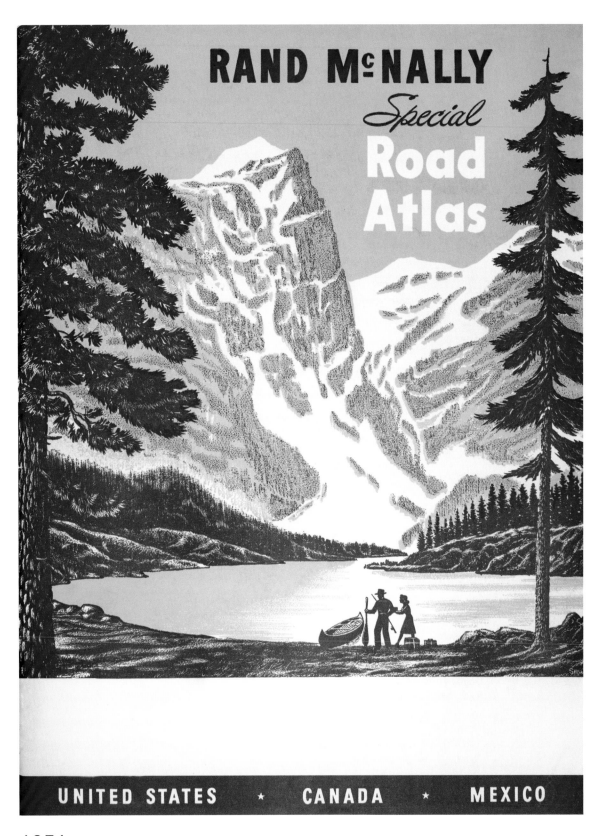

1951

1952

United States ★ Canada ★ Mexico

1954

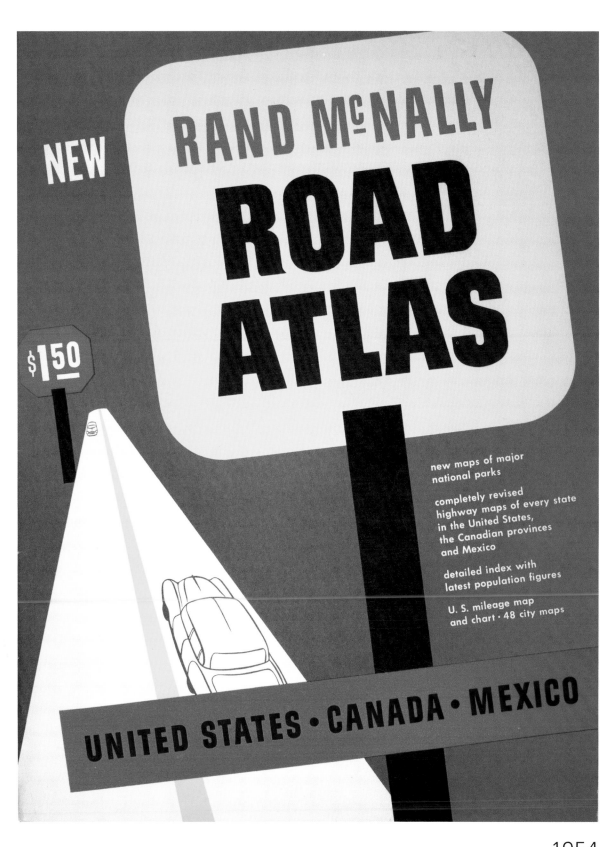

1954

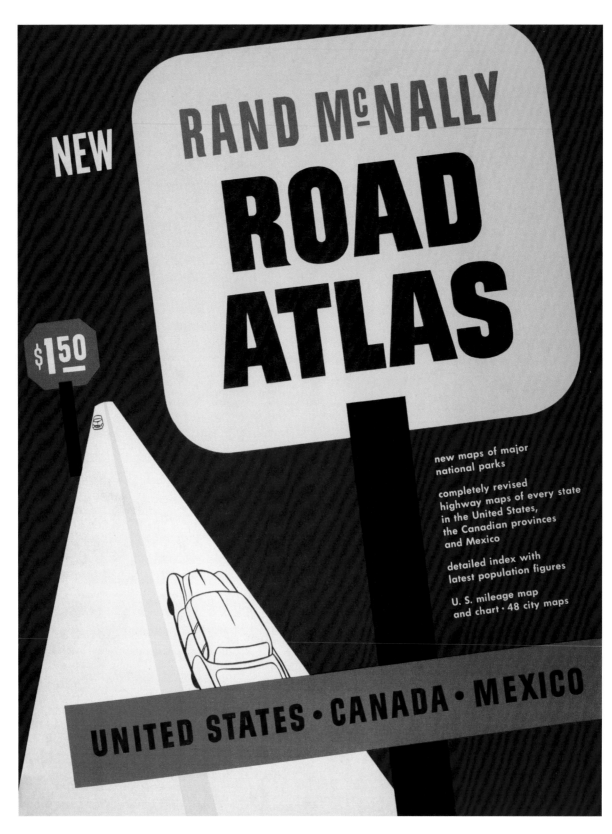

1955

$1.75

RAND McNALLY **ROAD ATLAS**

United States
Canada
Mexico

- completely new maps of every state

containing more detail than any other road atlas maps available

- special United States turnpike map

- latest and most complete turnpike information

- 118 pages of maps covering the United States, Canada and Mexico

- 147 city maps—15 national park maps

- 27 special state mileage charts

- U. S. highway mileage table

- U. S. highway mileage and driving time chart

- 1957 edition—completely up-to-date

1957

$1.75

RAND McNALLY **ROAD**

ATLAS

United States

Canada

Mexico

HOW TO USE THE NEW QUICK REFERENCE SIDE INDEX ▷

Refer to alphabetical list of state and province names on first page for map desired.

Roll back page with thumb until markings printed on the edge of the page are visible.

Locate the map you want by lining up the corresponding color marking on the edge of the page with the map title and color on the first page.

- **completely new maps** of every state
containing **more detail** than any other road atlas maps available
- **118 pages of maps** covering the United States, Canada and Mexico
- **147 city maps**—15 national park maps
- 27 special **state mileage charts**
- U. S. highway **mileage table**
- U. S. highway mileage and **driving time chart**

1958

Rand McNally Special

ROAD ATLAS

UNITED STATES   •   CANADA   •   MEXICO

1958

THE
1960s

Cheap fuel. Big cars. Big changes.

By 1960, 61 million cars were registered in the U.S. and interstate construction was booming. Gas was thirty cents a gallon while large luxury cars cost about $2,600. Young people were buying new cars; more than 600,000 Ford Mustangs were sold in 1966 alone. All of this car activity made touring, commuting, and "cruising" possible and popular.

Cartographers frequently updated maps to keep pace with the growing interstate system. Maps were now full color and included rest stops, national parks, and more. Some service stations offered customized, free maps with fill-ups, too!

Sixties design reflected pop art, optical art, and psychedelic influences. Rand McNally *Road Atlas* covers took cues from advertising and movie posters, favoring clear graphic communication in flat colors and iconic shapes. Graphics, and even type fonts, were image-filled to communicate more with less.

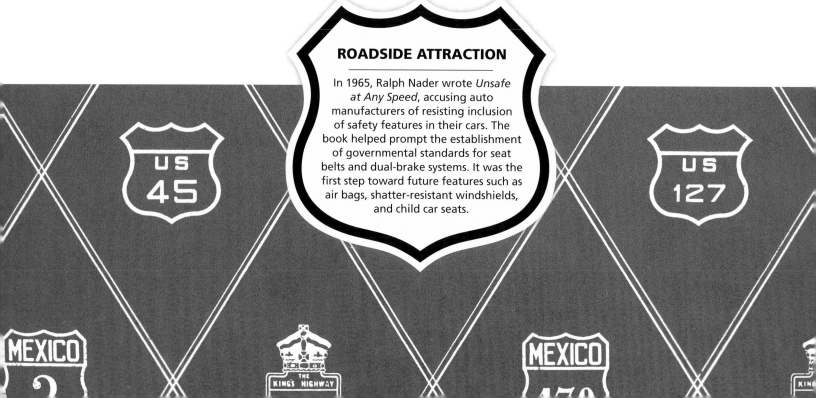

ROADSIDE ATTRACTION

In 1965, Ralph Nader wrote *Unsafe at Any Speed*, accusing auto manufacturers of resisting inclusion of safety features in their cars. The book helped prompt the establishment of governmental standards for seat belts and dual-brake systems. It was the first step toward future features such as air bags, shatter-resistant windshields, and child car seats.

RAND McNALLY **ROAD ATLAS**

UNITED STATES · CANADA · MEXICO

1960

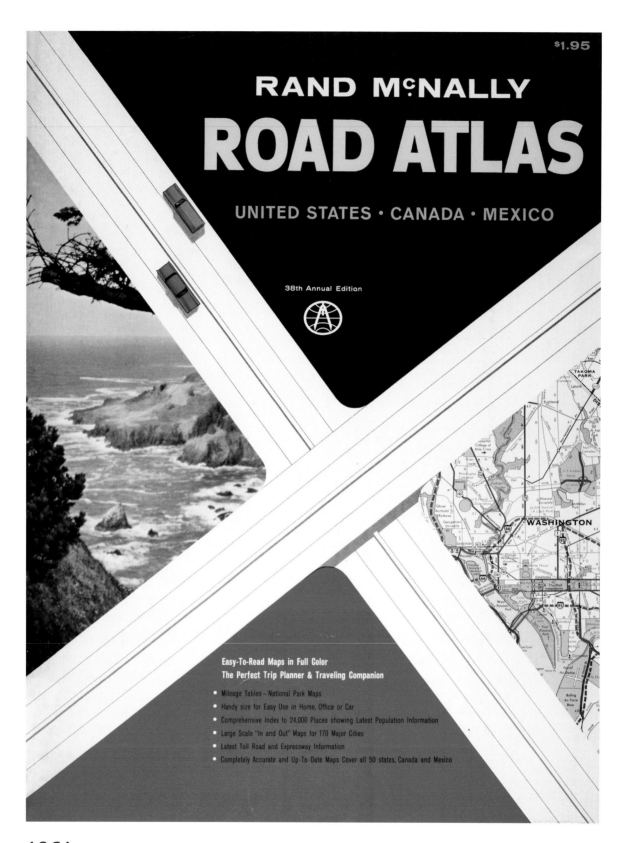

1961

RAND McNALLY

39TH ANNUAL EDITION

ROAD ATLAS

UNITED STATES · CANADA · MEXICO

$1.95

Easy-To-Read Maps in Full Color
The Perfect Trip Planner & Traveling Companion

- Mileage Tables – National Park Maps
- Handy size for Easy Use in Home, Office or Car
- Comprehensive Index to 24,000 Places showing Latest Population Information
- Large Scale "In and Out" Maps for 170 Major Cities
- Latest Toll Road and Expressway Information
- Completely Accurate and Up-To-Date Maps Cover all 50 states, Canada and Mexico

1963

$1.95

RAND McNALLY
ROAD ATLAS
40th
ANNUAL EDITION

UNITED STATES
CANADA · MEXICO

America's Favorite Road Guide featuring
Easy-To-Read Maps in Full Color

★ Full Color Mileage Table—Driving Time Chart

★ Completely Accurate and Up-To-Date Maps

★ Handy Size for Easy Use in Home, Office or Car

★ Comprehensive Index to 24,000 Places,
including Latest Population Figures

★ Latest Toll Road and Expressway Information

★ Large Scale Maps for 170 Major Cities
and 18 National Parks

1964

1965

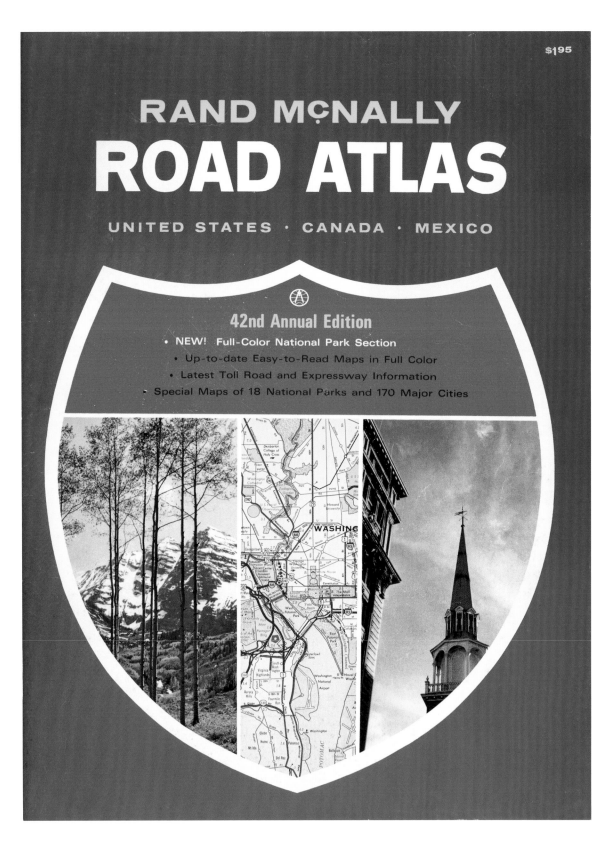

1966

1967

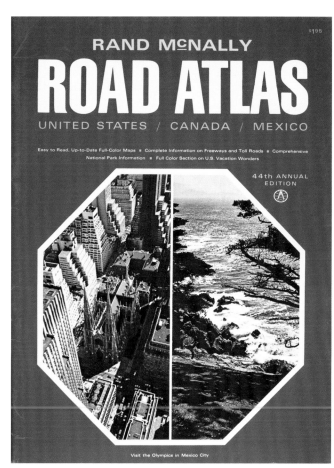

1968

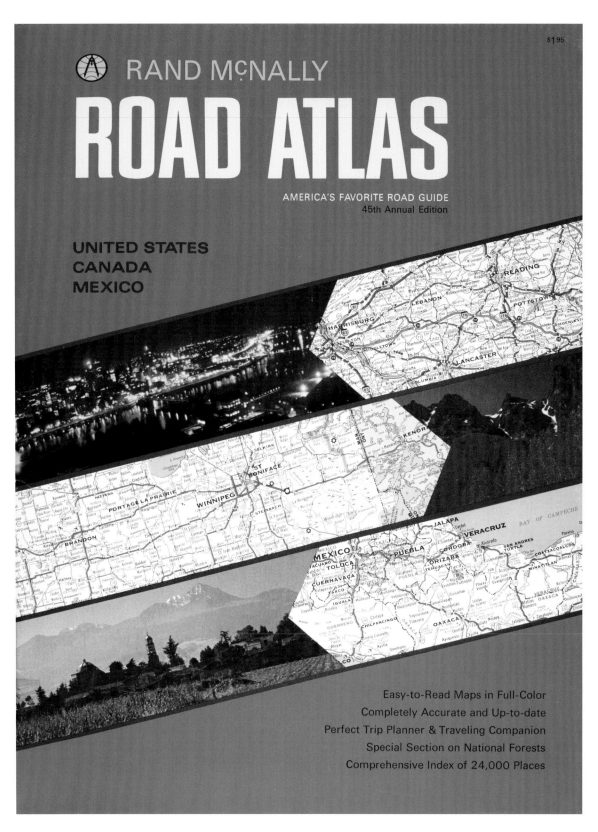

$1.95

RAND McNALLY
ROAD ATLAS

AMERICA'S FAVORITE ROAD GUIDE
45th Annual Edition

UNITED STATES
CANADA
MEXICO

Easy-to-Read Maps in Full-Color
Completely Accurate and Up-to-date
Perfect Trip Planner & Traveling Companion
Special Section on National Forests
Comprehensive Index of 24,000 Places

1969

Rand McNally

ROAD ATLAS

UNITED STATES · CANADA · MEXICO

1969

THE
1970s

Gas shortage. Speed limit. Economy cars.

America relied heavily upon foreign oil in the 1970s. When the Organization of the Petroleum Exporting Countries (OPEC) imposed an embargo, shortages ensued and the price of refined gasoline shot up to more than a dollar per gallon. As long lines at the pumps plagued drivers, Congress enacted a 55-mile-per-hour highway speed limit to curb gas consumption.

Americans turned to smaller, fuel-efficient cars from Japanese manufacturers. Commuter lanes offered drivers a fuel-saving way to get to work and hitchhikers were a common sight. Through it all, road trips stayed a popular way to vacation in the recession economy.

Photography drove *Road Atlas* design in the 1970s. Type and illustrations were mixed with photos and collages of color-enhanced images. Straightforward and efficient was the design, just like the cars travelers drove.

ROADSIDE ATTRACTION

In the 1970s, photographer John Margolies ramped up a 40-year mission to chronicle the America born of auto travel. His books and Roadside America Photograph Archive in the Library of Congress preserve the signs, kitsch, whimsical roadside structures, and quirky attractions that define American auto travel.

1970

Road Atlas

UNITED STATES / CANADA / MEXICO

AMERICA'S FAVORITE ROAD GUIDE
47th ANNUAL EDITION

New, Enlarged Special Feature Section
Latest Census Information / Revised and Updated Maps
Activities, Facilities and Accommodations at National Parks and Forests

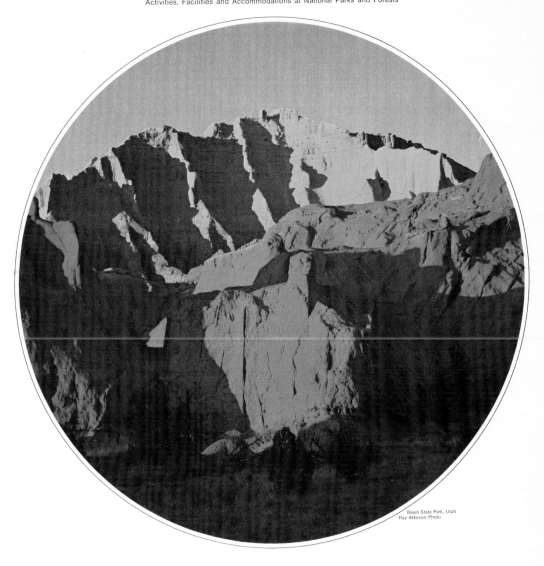

Basin State Park, Utah
Ray Atkeson Photo

1971

RAND MᶜNALLY
Road Atlas
UNITED STATES / CANADA / MEXICO

$2.⁹⁵

7 **NEW** State Maps / 11 **NEW** City Maps / **NEW** Canada Map / **NEW** Radio Station Log / **NEW** Mileage Tables

48th Annual Edition

1972

$2.95

RAND McNALLY

Road Atlas

UNITED STATES / CANADA / MEXICO

America's Favorite Road Guide / 49th Annual Edition

Revised and Updated Throughout / Final U.S. Census Figures in Index / Radio Station and Mileage Tables

1973

$2.95

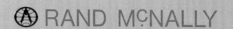 RAND MCNALLY

ROAD ATLAS

UNITED STATES / CANADA / MEXICO

America's Favorite Road Guide for Fifty Years
History of Road Maps / National Parks, Forests
New, easy-to-follow Scenic Route Markings

GOLDEN ANNIVERSARY EDITION

1974

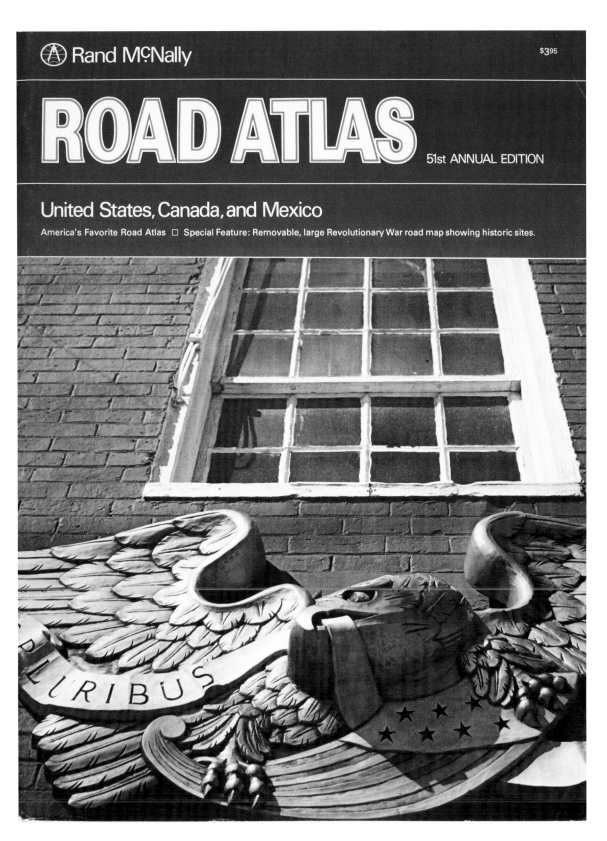

Rand McNally

$3⁹⁵

ROAD ATLAS

51st ANNUAL EDITION

United States, Canada, and Mexico

America's Favorite Road Atlas ☐ Special Feature: Removable, large Revolutionary War road map showing historic sites.

1975

1976

1977

$3.95

Rand McNally
ROAD ATLAS
UNITED STATES / CANADA / MEXICO

54th Annual Edition of America's favorite Road Guide

REVISED and UPDATED

1978

1979

THE
1980s

Commuters. American optimism. Family road trips.

In the 1980s, with relatively low fuel prices and increasingly efficient
cars, more travelers were on the road than ever before. Baby Boomers — those
born between 1946 and 1964 — moved to newly developed suburbs
via new roads, which fed into an interstate system that now connected
the country from coast to coast.

Renewed national pride made exploring the United States popular.
The family road trip was part of growing up in the eighties, and the
introduction of minivans made it all the more comfortable. Rand McNally
rolled with the times with more detailed maps that included
trip-saving coupons inside.

Crisp photos dominated Rand McNally *Road Atlas* covers, showcasing
America's beauty in big, bold hues and letting the image sell the adventure.
American imagery dominated the covers, reflecting renewed national
pride that made exploring the United States popular.

ROADSIDE ATTRACTION

After spending years developing
a small affordable van that
handled more like a car, Chrysler
in the early 1980s unveiled the
minivan. The family oriented
minivan went on to replace the
station wagon as the large
passenger car of choice.

1980

1981

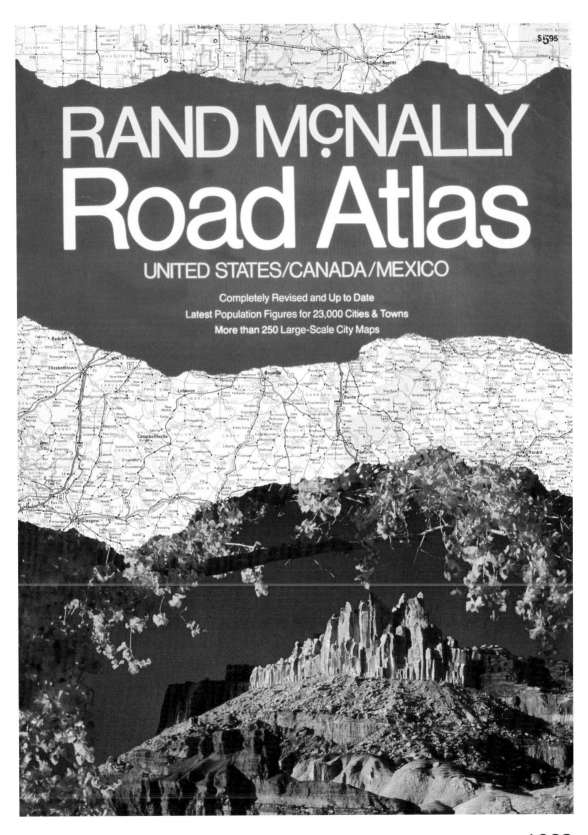

RAND McNALLY
Road Atlas
UNITED STATES/CANADA/MEXICO

Completely Revised and Up to Date
Latest Population Figures for 23,000 Cities & Towns
More than 250 Large-Scale City Maps

$5.95

1982

$5⁹⁵

Rand McNally
ROAD
ATLAS

UNITED STATES / CANADA / MEXICO

- America's Favorite Road Atlas for Traveling and Planning
- Revised and Updated
- Individual State and Province Maps
- More than 250 Detailed City Maps
- Charts Showing 11,000 Mileages Between Places
- Lists of 1,200 Points of Interest
- Index with Census Populations for 23,000 Places
- Mileage and Driving Time Map

1983

$5⁹⁵

🜨 Rand McNally

ROAD ATLAS

UNITED STATES · CANADA · MEXICO

- Mileage and driving-time map
- Easy to use for traveling and planning
- Detailed state and province maps
- More than 250 detailed city maps

- 60th Anniversary Edition
- Charts showing 11,000 mileages
- More than 18,000 revisions
- America's favorite road atlas

1984

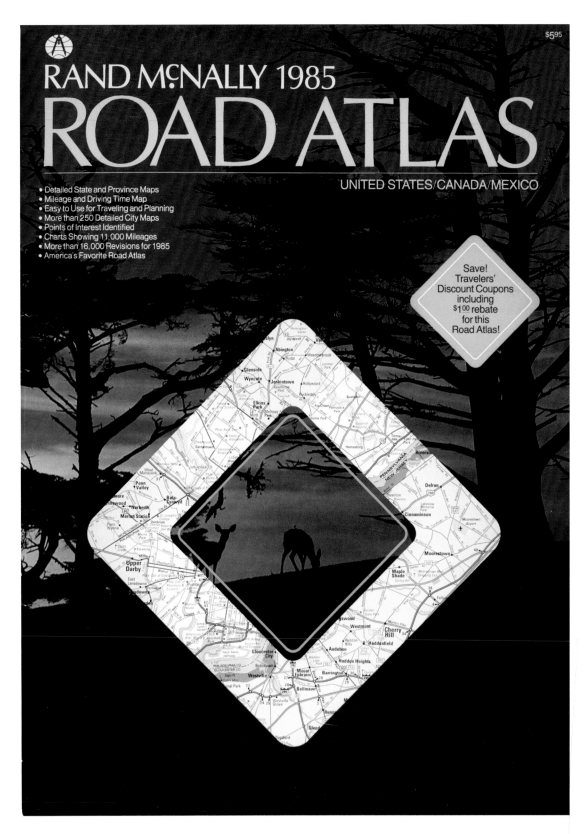

1985

1986

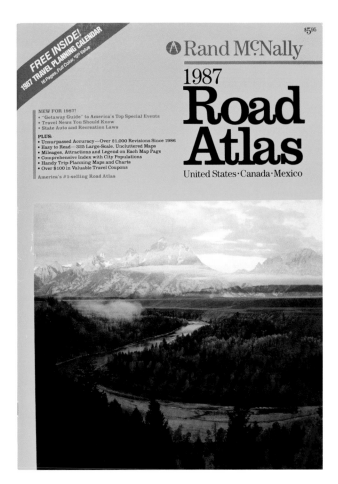

1987

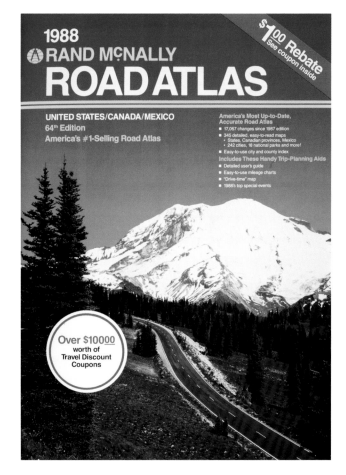

1988

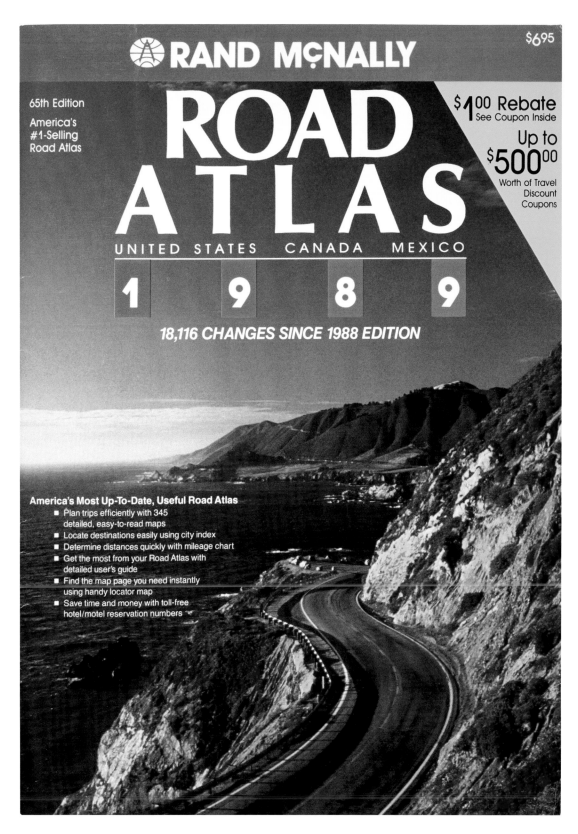

1989

THE
1990s

SUVs zoom. Technology booms.

In the 1990s, 80 percent of U.S. travel was by car. Beyond the minivan, the sport utility vehicle market ramped up. SUVs were made bigger and tougher to handle terrain outside urban and suburban areas, although many were filled with kids heading to the local soccer field.

Auto technology made giant strides. Life-saving airbags, onboard diagnostics, LED headlamps, and smart keys debuted. Cartography and Geographic Information Systems (GIS) technology accelerated, too. The 1993 edition of the Rand McNally *Road Atlas* was made using all-digital mapmaking methods.

It was a digital design decade — computers were used for design and typesetting. Professional digital cameras captured and stored photos. Printing from film was replaced with digital processes. Covers at the time reflected a more magazine-like feel with bits of copy and beautiful landscape photos.

ROADSIDE ATTRACTION

The color green – including teal, forest, aqua, all shades – became very popular in the nineties. Green was a favored color for cars as well. Later research would show that green cars tend to be less safe because they blend in with terrain, especially at dusk.

1990

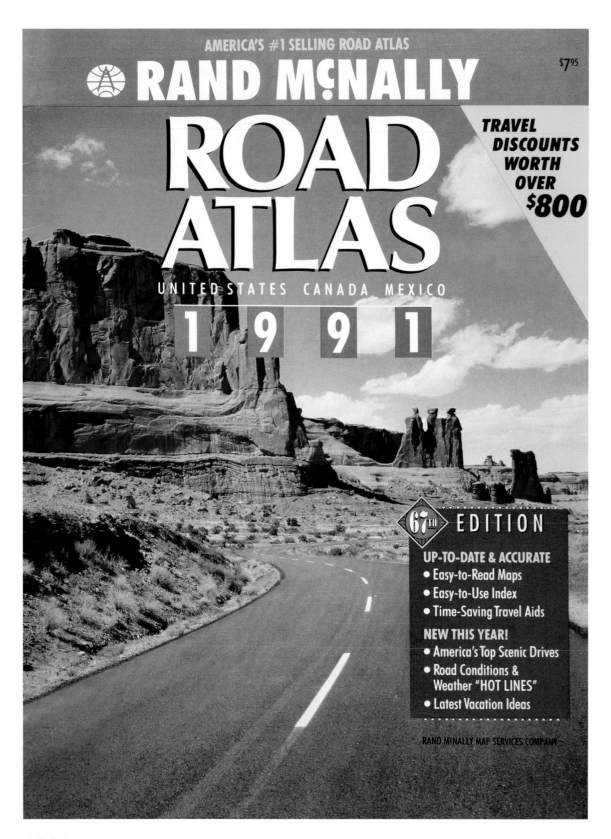

1991

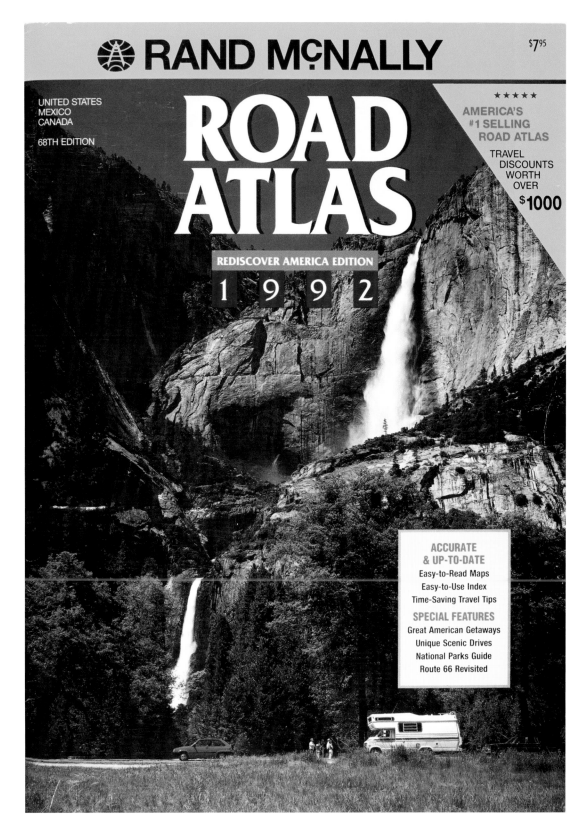

1992

1993

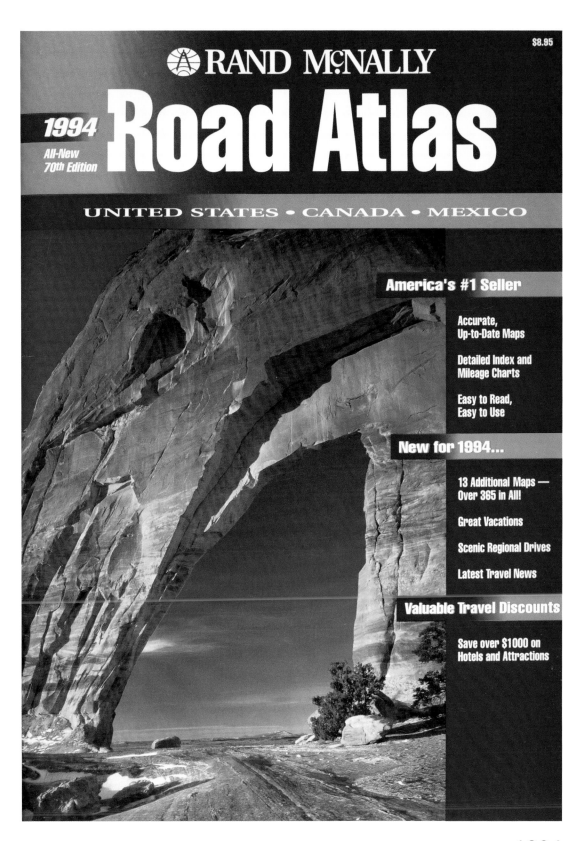

$8.95

RAND McNALLY

1994 Road Atlas

All-New 70th Edition

UNITED STATES • CANADA • MEXICO

America's #1 Seller

Accurate, Up-to-Date Maps

Detailed Index and Mileage Charts

Easy to Read, Easy to Use

New for 1994...

13 Additional Maps — Over 365 in All!

Great Vacations

Scenic Regional Drives

Latest Travel News

Valuable Travel Discounts

Save over $1000 on Hotels and Attractions

1994

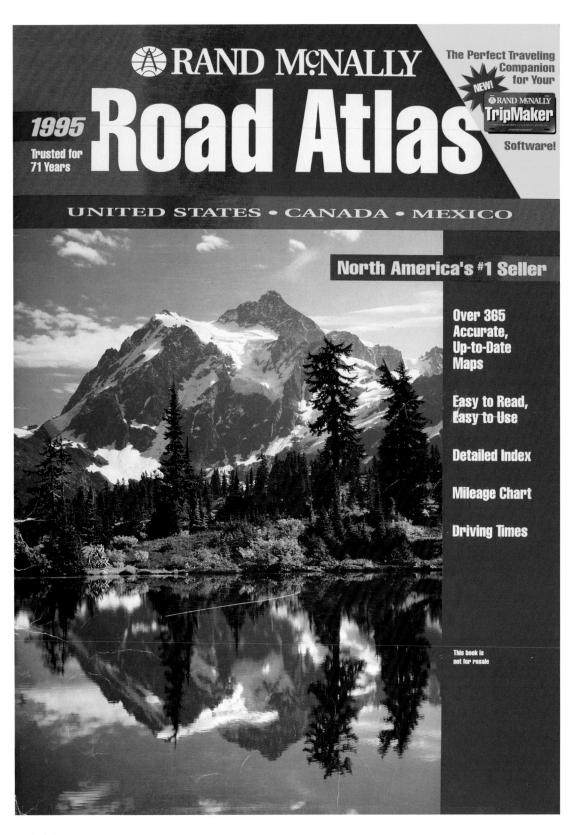

1995

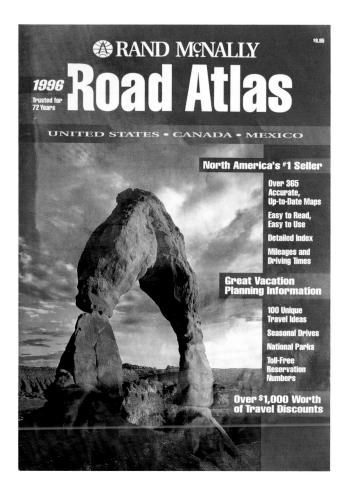

1996

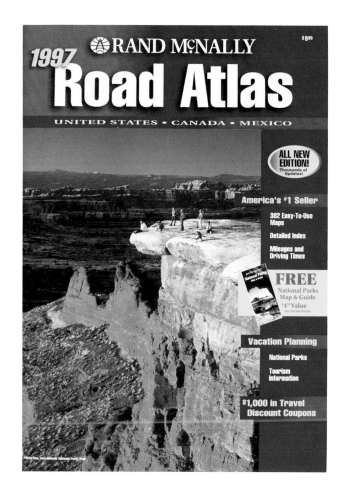

1997

1998

1999

THE
2000s

More time on the road. Keeping up with drivers.

By 2001, it was estimated that commuters spent close to an hour driving to and from work each day.

Since American families and workers were in the car more than ever, the auto industry introduced technology to deliver better performance, fuel efficiency, and a safer ride. Rand McNally kept up with the times, releasing a maps and directions app for wireless phones.

Advanced software allowed designers to create more expressive and communicative covers. Rand McNally focused imagery on the "destination" for vacationers and introduced the distinctive yellow that identifies the atlas to this day.

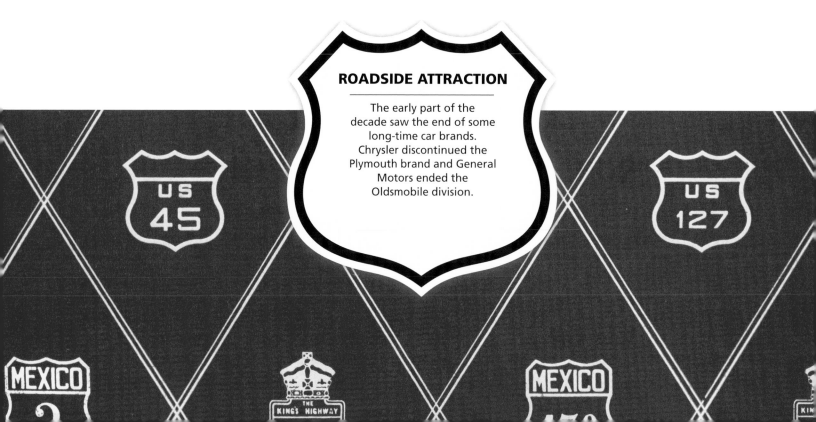

ROADSIDE ATTRACTION

The early part of the decade saw the end of some long-time car brands. Chrysler discontinued the Plymouth brand and General Motors ended the Oldsmobile division.

2000

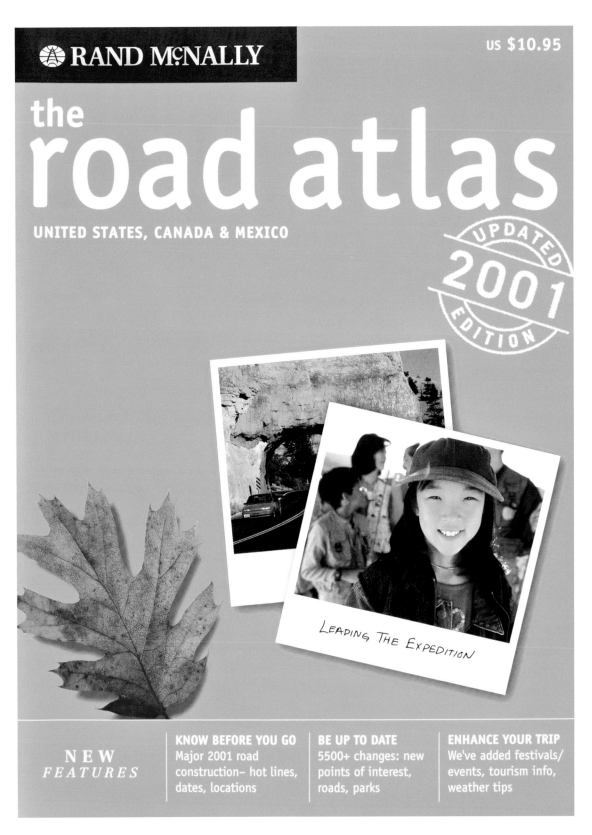

US $10.95

RAND McNALLY

the
road atlas

UNITED STATES, CANADA & MEXICO

UPDATED
2001
EDITION

LEADING THE EXPEDITION

NEW
FEATURES

KNOW BEFORE YOU GO
Major 2001 road
construction– hot lines,
dates, locations

BE UP TO DATE
5500+ changes: new
points of interest,
roads, parks

ENHANCE YOUR TRIP
We've added festivals/
events, tourism info,
weather tips

2001

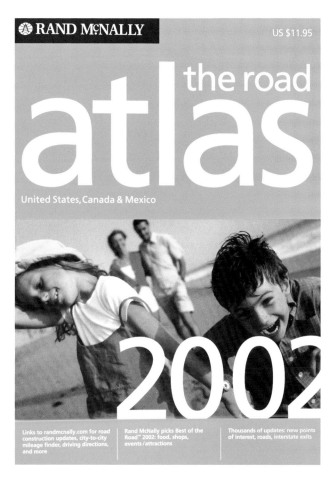

2002

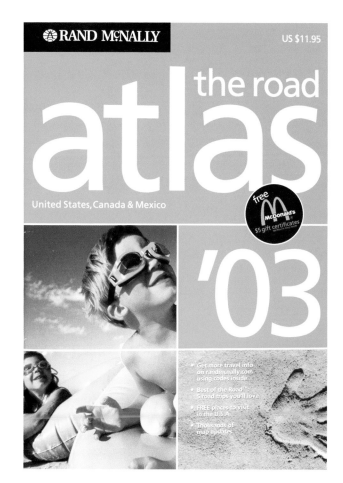

2003

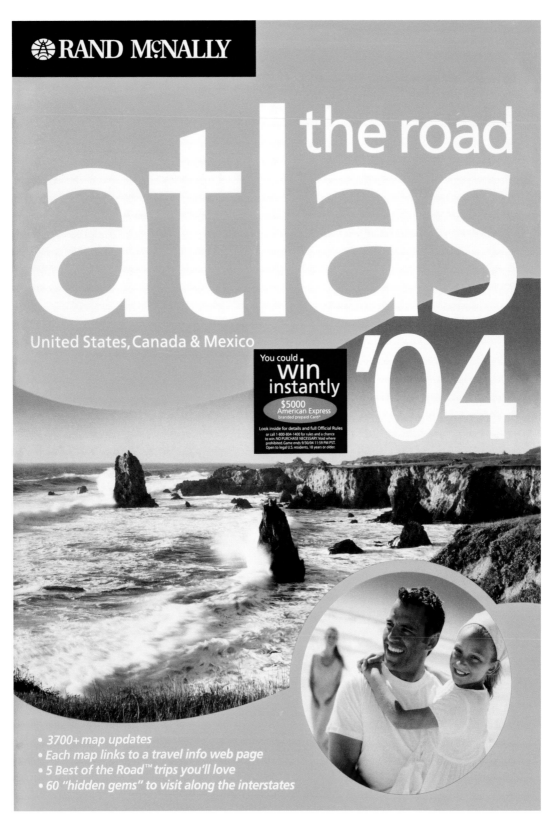

RAND McNALLY

the road
atlas
United States, Canada & Mexico
'04

You could **win instantly**

$5000
American Express
branded prepaid Card*

Look inside for details and full Official Rules
or call 1-800-804-1400 for rules and a chance
to win. NO PURCHASE NECESSARY. Void where
prohibited. Game ends 9/30/04 11:59 PM PST.
Open to legal U.S. residents, 18 years or older.

- 3700+ map updates
- Each map links to a travel info web page
- 5 Best of the Road™ trips you'll love
- 60 "hidden gems" to visit along the interstates

2004

RAND MCNALLY

FREE
road construction
updates
— see back cover

the road
atlas
'05

America's
#1 Road
Atlas

INCLUDES:

U.S., Canada, Mexico

5,100+ map updates

Toll-free hotel and
tourism numbers

5 Best of the Road™
trips you'll love

Exclusive page codes
link to online travel info

Plus 329 city maps

La Jolla, California

2005

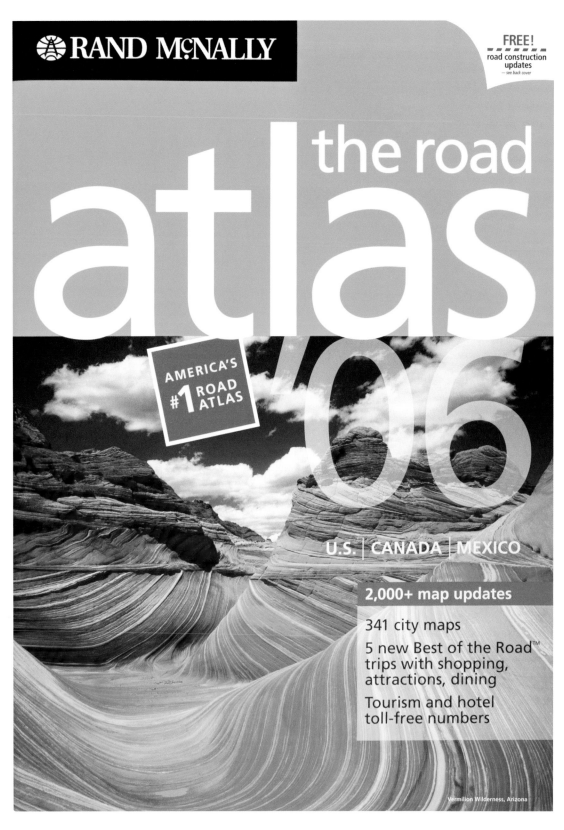

2006

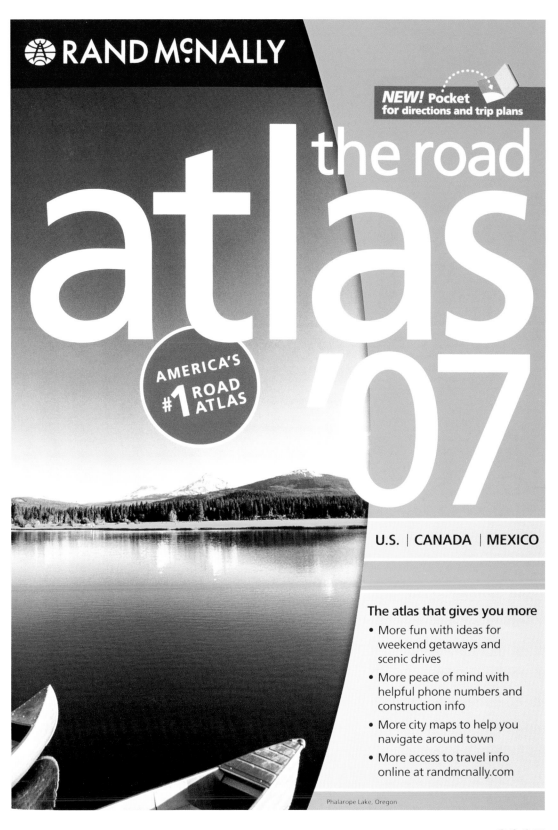

2007

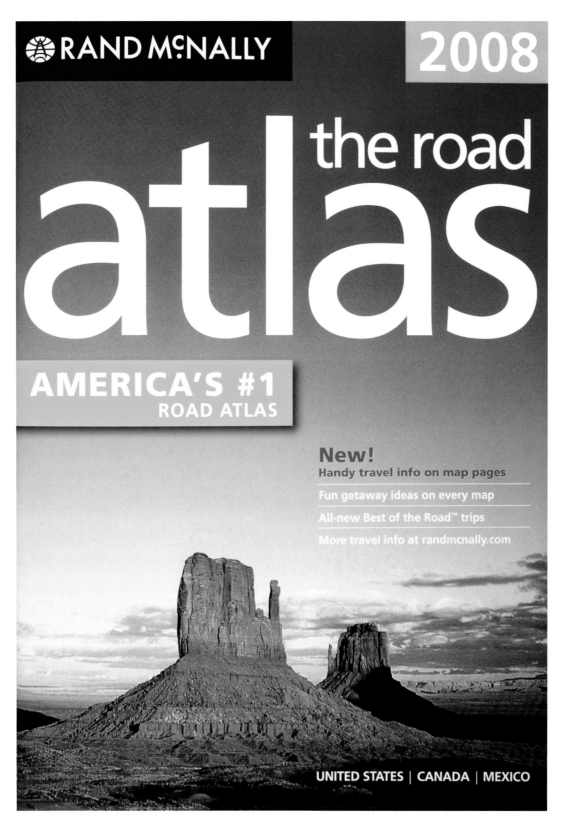

2008

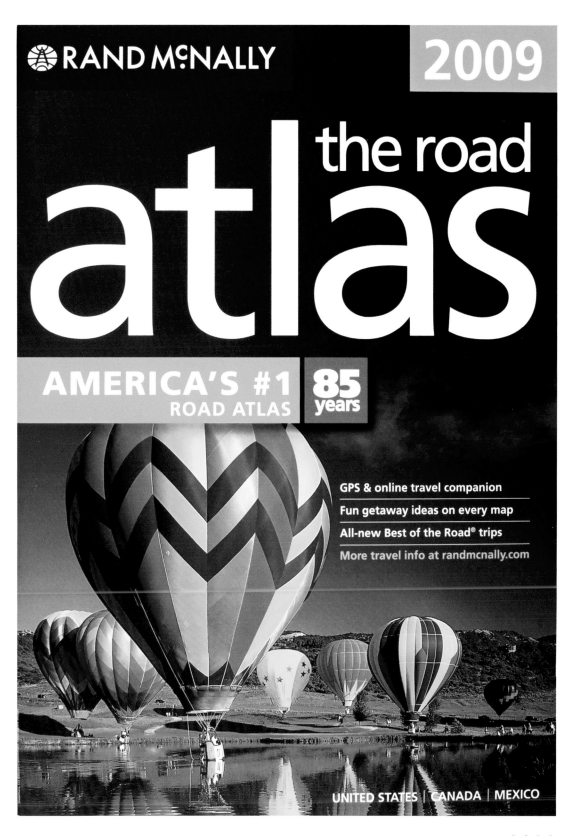

2009

THE
2010s

Living while driving. Still journeying.

Technology continued to drive the auto industry. In-car Wi-Fi and Bluetooth technology gave drivers and passengers more options to connect than ever before. Amid all of the smart technology, the old-school family road trip still thrives. Although in-car navigation is plentiful, the Rand McNally *Road Atlas* is still used for planning travels and serving as a back-up on the road – no batteries required.

Road Atlas covers during this decade showcased beautiful landscapes and national parks in high-resolution, full bleed photos – providing visual inspiration for hopping in the car and hitting the road.

ROADSIDE ATTRACTION

There are more than 4 million miles of road in the United States, according to the U.S. Department of Transportation. This distance is equivalent to traveling from Earth to the Moon about 17 times.

2010

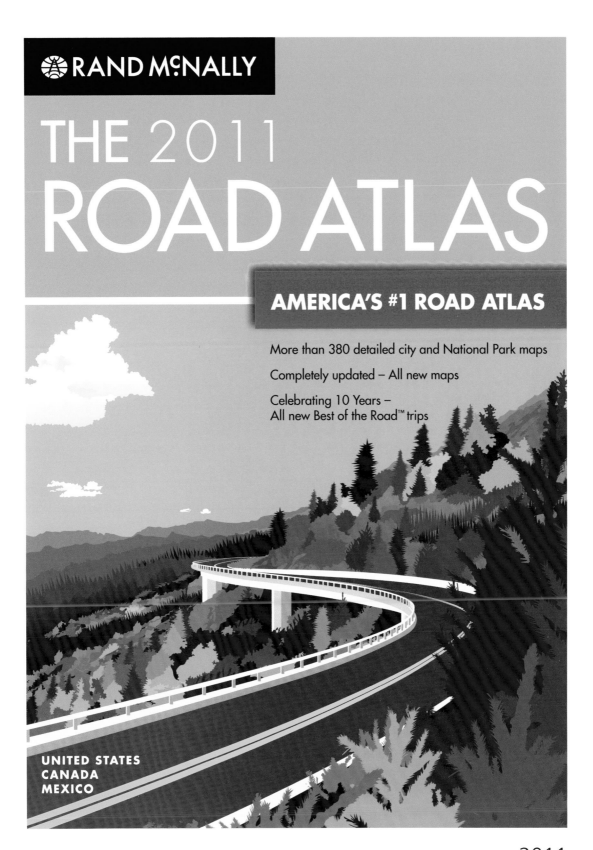

2011

2012

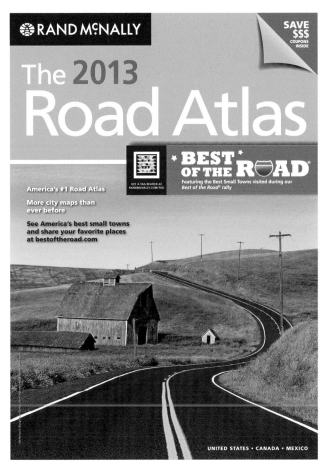

2013

2014

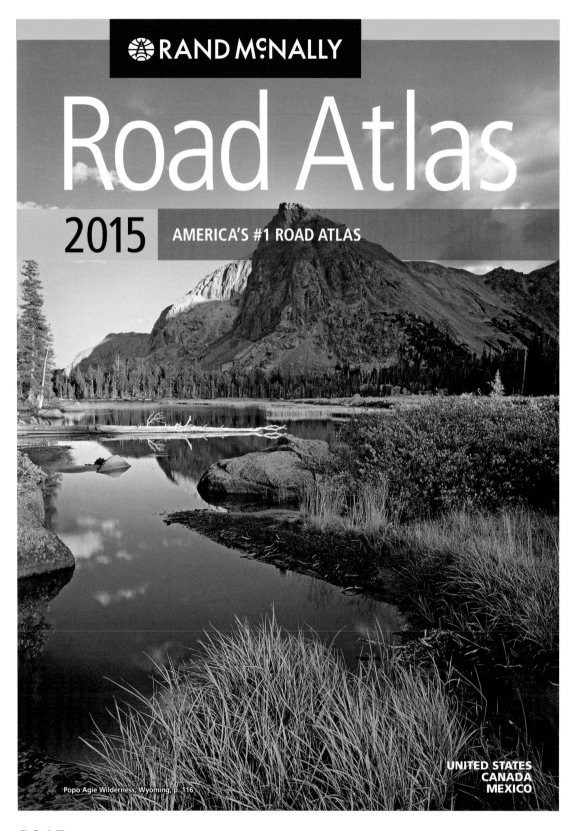

RAND MCNALLY

Road Atlas

2015 AMERICA'S #1 ROAD ATLAS

Popo Agie Wilderness, Wyoming, p. 116

UNITED STATES
CANADA
MEXICO

2015

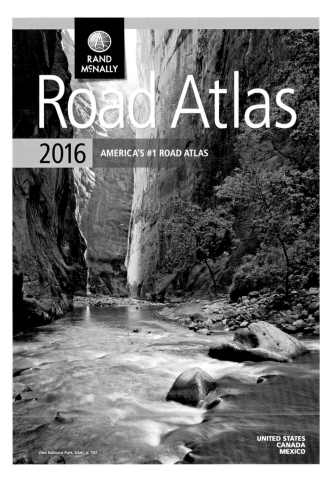

2016

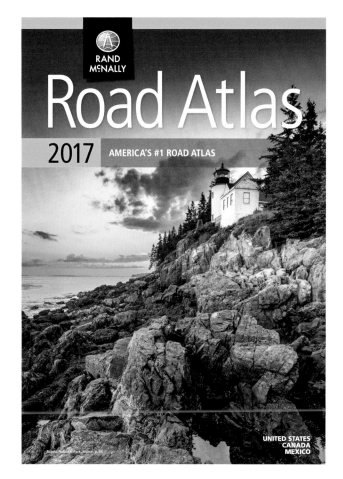

2017

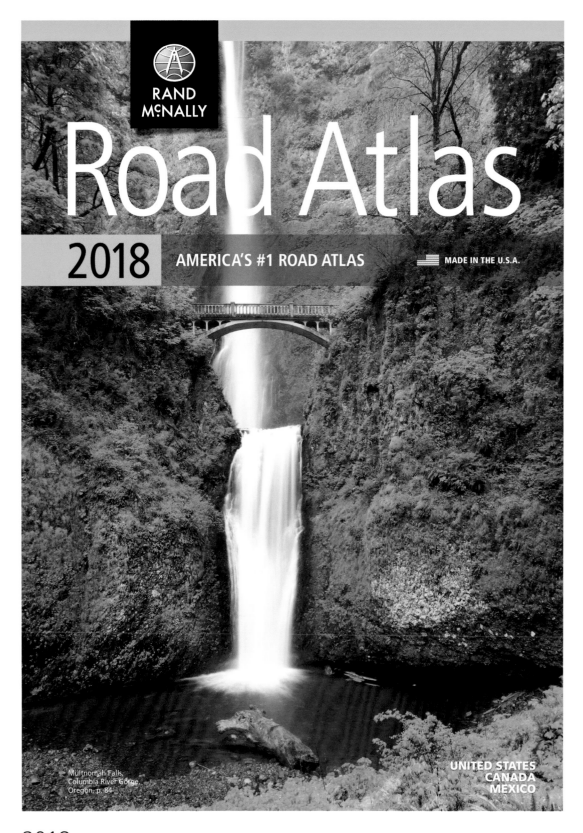

RAND McNALLY

Road Atlas

2018 AMERICA'S #1 ROAD ATLAS

MADE IN THE U.S.A.

Multnomah Falls,
Columbia River Gorge
Oregon, p. 84

UNITED STATES
CANADA
MEXICO

2018

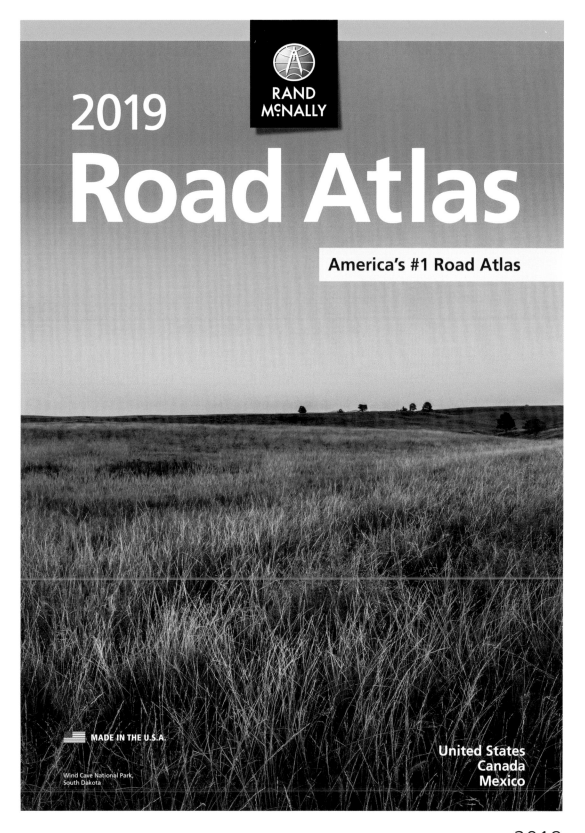

2019 **Road Atlas**

America's #1 Road Atlas

MADE IN THE U.S.A.

Wind Cave National Park,
South Dakota

United States
Canada
Mexico

2019

Publisher: **Joan Sharp**

Writer: **Mary Bunker**

Editor: **Alison Kerr Miller**

Design Director: **Joerg Metzner**

Art Director: **Jodie Knight**

Design Production: **Joe Rockey**

Product Management Director: **Jenny Thornton**

Production: **Carey Seren**